D0742469

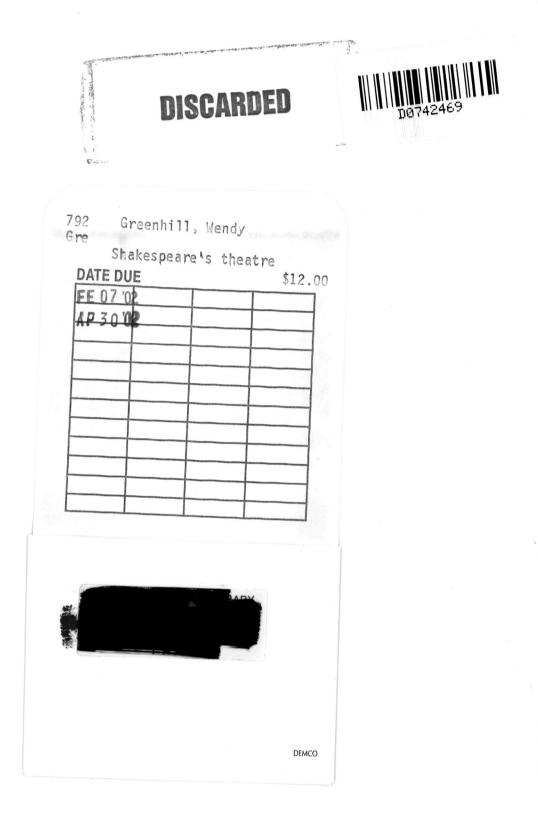

792
Gre

Greenhill, Wendy

Shakespeare's theatre

DATE DUE $12.00

FE 07 '02			
AP 30 '02			

DEMCO

Shakespeare's Theatre

WENDY GREENHILL

HEAD OF EDUCATION,
ROYAL SHAKESPEARE COMPANY

Heinemann Library,
an imprint of Heinemann Publishers (Oxford) Ltd,
Halley Court, Jordan Hill, Oxford, England, OX2 8EJ.

OXFORD LONDON EDINBURGH MADRID PARIS
ATHENS BOLOGNA MELBOURNE SYDNEY
AUCKLAND SINGAPORE TOKYO IBADAN
NAIROBI GABORONE HARARE PORTSMOUTH NH (USA)

First published 1995
95 96 97 10 9 8 7 6 5 4 3 2 1

British Library Cataloguing in Publication Data
Greenhill, Wendy
'Shakespeare's Theatre'.-(Shakespeare Library)
I. Title II. Series
822. 33

ISBN 0 431 07550 6

Designed by Green Door Design Ltd
Printed and bound in Hong Kong

Acknowledgements
The authors and publishers would like to thank the following for
permission to reproduce photographs:
Bibl. Universitat de Utrecht p7 British Library pp4, 23, 26 Marquess of
Bath p21 Museum of London p9 Richard Kalina p28 Shakespeare
Centre p29 The Governors of Dulwich College p8 The Honourable
Society of the Middle Temple p16 The Master and Fellows of Magdalene
College, Cambridge p20 The Provost and Fellows of Worcester College,
Oxford p18 The Trustees of Dulwich Picture Gallery p12

CONTENTS

INTRODUCTION

WILLIAM SHAKESPEARE

William Shakespeare was born in Stratford upon Avon in 1564. At the age of eighteen he married Anne Hathaway who had three children. Shakespeare then moved to London, apparently leaving his family behind. He worked in the London theatres during the 1590s as writer, actor and co-manager of a company of actors and of a theatre building.

Shakespeare earned enough money at this time to buy the second largest house in Stratford – New Place. His wife and children moved there in 1597. From then until his death in 1616 Shakespeare spent more time in Stratford, although he still wrote plays which were performed in London.

POETS – PLAYERS – COMPANIES

In Shakespeare's day playwrights were called **poets**, actors were known as **players**, and theatres were **playhouses**. Shakespeare was one of several extremely gifted and outsize personalities of his time. They transformed the theatre from a travelling entertainment, where groups of players set up rough stages in inn yards or market places, to a fully professional activity in purpose-built theatres in the capital city, London. Players were forbidden by law to

Engraving of William Shakespeare by Martin Droeshout, 1623.

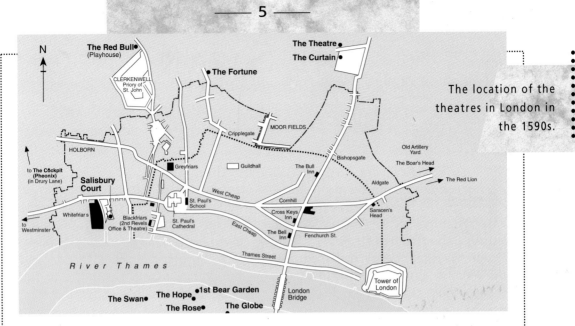

N

The Red Bull (Playhouse)

The Theatre
The Curtain

The Fortune

CLERKENWELL Priory of St. John

The location of the theatres in London in the 1590s.

MOOR FIELDS

Cripplegate

HOLBORN

Bishopsgate

Old Artillery Yard

The Boar's Head

to **The Cockpit** (Pheonix) (in Drury Lane)

Salisbury Court

Greyfriars

Guildhall

The Bull Inn

Aldgate

The Red Lion

West Cheap

Cornhill

Saracen's Head

Whitefriars

St. Paul's School

Cross Keys Inn

to Westminster

Blackfriars (2nd Revels Office & Theatre)

St. Paul's Cathedral

East Cheap

The Bell Inn

Fenchurch St.

Thames Street

River Thames

Tower of London

The Swan

The Hope **1st Bear Garden**

The Rose **The Globe**

London Bridge

travel around as unattached entertainers and had to form themselves into companies under the protection of a nobleman. Shakespeare worked for several different companies before becoming a co-manager and shareholder in the **Chamberlain's Men**. When James I became king in 1603 after the death of Queen Elizabeth, Shakespeare's company became the **King's Men**.

PLAYHOUSES

The first purpose-built theatre was probably the **Red Lion**, built in Whitechapel in 1567. In 1576 it was replaced by the **Theatre** in Shoreditch, built in a prominent position on one of the main roads going north out of the city.

The man behind the Theatre was **James Burbage**. In 1599 his sons Cuthbert and Richard used its timbers as the frame for the **Globe**, one of several theatres on the south bank of the Thames, still known as Bankside. The **Rose** (1587), the

Swan (1595), the **Hope** (1614) and a second **Globe** (1614) were all on Bankside, with the **Fortune** (1600) and the **Curtain** (1577) to the north, and the **Red Bull**, converted from an inn in 1604, in Clerkenwell to the north-west.

AUDIENCES

Performances were given every afternoon, Monday to Saturday. A fine day and a popular play would pack in a large, mixed audience of up to about 3000 people. For one penny you could stand in the yard next to the stage with hundreds of others. **Thomas Dekker**, another playwright, complained of being crowded next to 'garlic-breathed stinkards'. A higher price bought a seat in one of the galleries.

We know from contemporary accounts that the audience in these first playhouses included apprentices, tradesmen, ambassadors and other foreign visitors, scholars and noblemen. In the 1590s everyone went to the theatre.

THE SWAN

In 1589 **Francis Langley**, a successful London goldsmith, bought land south of the Thames. In 1595 or 1596 he built a theatre there. In 1596 a Dutch visitor to London, **Johannes de Witt**, described the **playhouses** in his diary, and Francis Langley's **Swan** seems to have been his favourite:

> *'There are four amphitheatres in London of notable beauty ... In them a different play is presented daily to the people. The two finest of these are situated to the south west beyond the Thames ... Of all the theatres however the largest and most distinguished is that of which the sign is a swan ... since it has seating accommodation for three thousand persons, and is built of a mass of flint stones and supported by wooden columns painted in ... excellent imitation of marble ... I have made a drawing of it.'*

A copy of de Witt's sketch was made by his friend **Arend van Buchell** in 1596 but was not discovered until 1888.

De Witt's diary and drawing provide us with a lot of evidence of what the playhouses looked like and how they were used. We can see clearly the circular shape of the building, the open roof, and the stage with space for an audience on three sides – some spectators in the galleries, some standing in the yard. There are other interesting details – for example, the flag flying and someone blowing a trumpet in the tower. Perhaps this showed that a performance was about to begin, or was already under way. The three **players** seem to be dressed in clothes of their own time. They are well to the front of the stage. At the back is a covered area with two double doors for entrances. There are people sitting in the gallery above the stage. They might be members of the audience or musicians. It is likely that this gallery was also sometimes used as an acting area: many plays written for the playhouses seem to need a room or space 'above'. Juliet's balcony in *Romeo and Juliet* is a famous example.

The Swan had a chequered career. The company which used it first, the **Earl of Pembroke's Men**, staged a play called *The Isle of Dogs* which angered the Privy Council. It was condemned as 'contanynge very seditious and slanderous matter'. In other words, it criticized the authorities. The Queen's Privy Council immediately closed all the public playhouses, and those responsible for the play were imprisoned. For the remainder of Elizabeth's reign only two companies were officially approved.

This incident shows us that the playhouses were thought to have a powerful effect on public opinion. They were places full of dangerous ideas as well as popular entertainment.

A drawing of the Swan made in 1596 by a Dutch visitor to the London theatres.

THE ROSE

Even more detailed evidence has survived about how the **Rose** (1587) was built and run. Its owner and manager, **Philip Henslowe**, kept an account book and record of his business affairs which explains many of the financial arrangements of the theatre. Henslowe entered into a Deed of Agreement with **John**

Cholmley, a grocer. Cholmley was to pay a certain amount four times a year in return for which he could sell refreshments to the audience. He was entitled to keep the profits from the sale of 'any breade or drinke'. Henslowe paid for the construction of the theatre but they agreed to share the job of finding the 'players to use, exersyse and playe in the saide playe howse'. They also intended to be present at performances so that each could keep an eye on the amount of money taken, which they split fifty-fifty. In fact their money would only have been half that raised by the sale of the gallery seats. The other half, and the penny-per-head of those in the yard, went to the **players**.

From 1592, Henslowe's players at the Rose included **Edward Alleyn**, a leading actor, who had great success in the first performances of **Christopher Marlowe's** plays, *Dr Faustus*, *Tamburlaine* and *The Jew of Malta*. Shakespeare's play, *Titus Andronicus*, had its first performance there in 1592 so it is possible that Alleyn would have played the title part.

Edward Alleyn, a leading actor with the Henslowe players. This painting was made in 1626.

In 1989 a team of archaeologists from the Museum of London unearthed the foundations of the Rose. They show that the walls formed a polygon, a many-sided building on the outside which makes the inside very nearly a circle. Five years after he first built it Henslowe improved the Rose by adding a roof over the stage area (like that shown in the de Witt drawing of the **Swan**). The new roof, and that over the galleries, was thatched. He also made his playhouse bigger by moving the stage back by 6 feet 6 inches (2 metres).

The rebuilding came at the time when Edward Alleyn was about to join the company. It shows Henslowe's confidence that he could now attract much bigger audiences than before.

The excavation of the stage has also suggested that the Rose had a different shaped stage from other theatres. It was 18 feet (5.5 metres) deep (from front to back) and tapered in width from 36 feet (11 metres) to about 20 feet (6 metres). Our understanding of the measurements of the stage of the **Globe** suggests that it was about 40 feet (12 metres) deep from front to back. A drawing still exists of a performance of *Titus Andronicus* at the Rose. It shows the players standing in a line across the stage. The actors must often have done this, using the wide back-stage area for important moments involving many characters.

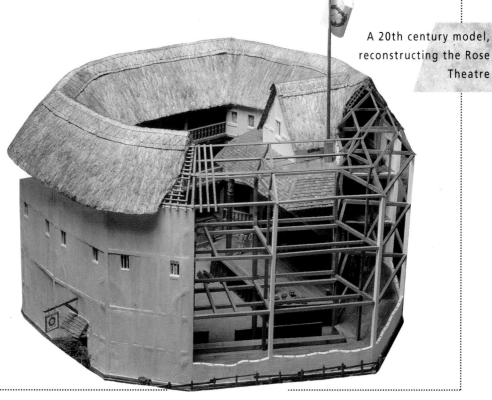

A 20th century model, reconstructing the Rose Theatre

THE FORTUNE

For twelve years the Rose had done well on Bankside, attracting playgoers who crossed London Bridge or took a boat over the Thames to see the great actor Alleyn in tragic or spectacular roles. Philip Henslowe and Alleyn both made a nice little fortune. Alleyn retired from the stage and devoted himself to good works, including founding Dulwich College, which remains as a school up to the present day.

Their success was partly because the only serious rival to the Rose, the Theatre run by James Burbage and a group of players including Shakespeare, was at a safe distance north of the river. In 1599 the competition between the two establishments hotted up: Burbage's sons had pulled down the Theatre and carried its timbers across the river to Bankside. They had employed an architect, Peter Street, to build a fine new playhouse, nearly within spitting distance of Henslowe's Rose. The new **Globe** was obviously a serious threat because Alleyn came out of retirement and took on a lease of land north of the Thames in Cripplegate. He and Henslowe made a cunning move in getting Peter Street to build them a playhouse with all the Globe's best features. The **Fortune** was to be a state-of-the-art theatre to re-establish the Henslowe-Alleyn reputation.

The Fortune opened in 1600. It gained a reputation for being rough, attracting pickpockets and troublemakers. One of these was Marion Frith who liked to dress as a man, which gave her the freedom to go where she liked and do as she pleased in the taverns and playhouses of London. On one occasion she shocked respectable Londoners by a surprise appearance on stage at a performance of a play by **Thomas Dekker** and **Thomas Middleton**, *The Roaring Girl*, based on her own life. A church court accused her of immoral behaviour, giving as an example an incident which doesn't seem so shocking today:

'... she sat upon the stage in public viewe of all the people ... in man's apparel and played upon her lute and sange a song.'

It was another 50 years before actresses were accepted on stage in London to play women's parts.

The building contract for the Fortune still exists and shows that it was a square building, unlike the others. It had three storeys and 'gentlemen's roomes', special boxes for the higher-paying members of the audience. The stage was backed by a tiring-house and its tower provided a space from which pieces of scenery, and perhaps even people, could be lowered. This was called the **Heavens**.

An illustration of an Elizabethan playhouse showing the different levels which could be used for special effects including a player lowered from the 'Heavens'.

THE FIRST GLOBE

In 1598 the famous actor and theatre manager, **Richard Burbage**, had a problem. His father had taken out a lease on land to the north of the city on which he had built the **Theatre**, one of the first and most successful of London's **playhouses**. The company of actors which played there, the **Chamberlain's Men**, included Shakespeare, who shared in the running of the theatre and its profits. As the lease came to an end the landowner made it plain that he would not renew it. Burbage made a brilliant and daring plan. On 28 December 1598 he, his brother Cuthbert, and twelve workmen, set to with axes and crowbars. Dismantling the Theatre plank by plank, they transported the timbers across the Thames to Bankside. The river was frozen over that winter, so perhaps they pushed everything over the ice!

The **Globe** which Peter Street built for Burbage, Shakespeare and their colleagues must be the most productive piece of recycling in history. At least 29 plays were written for the Chamberlain's Men (later known as the **King's Men**) during their first ten years at the Globe. Shakespeare gave them sixteen plays and it was in this playhouse that his great tragedies were staged, with Richard Burbage in the leading roles. Plays for the company by other writers have also passed the test of time and are still performed around the world today, 400 years after their opening at the Globe. These include plays by **Ben Jonson**, in which Shakespeare acted, and by **Thomas Dekker**.

The actor Richard Burbage was the first to play many of the major roles in Shakespeare's plays including Richard III, Hamlet, King Lear and Othello. This is probably a self portrait.

There is not much hard evidence about the structure of the Globe but scholars have deduced a certain amount from the plays which were written for it.

It took six months to build, was round or polygonal on the outside and more or less round inside. The galleries had a thatched roof, which proved disastrous in 1613 when a piece of smoking wadding from a cannon used in a performance of *Henry VIII* flew across from the stage corner and set fire to it. The fire burned the Globe to the ground.

In its brief life the Globe must have been a lively place to visit. Its stage stretched well into the yard, bringing actors and audience close together; it had a large trapdoor and, above the stage, the **Heavens**. The **tiring-house** at the back was an arrangement of front wall with a door at each side for entrances, and a central alcove obscured either by a curtain or double doors. There was also an upper playing space provided by the gallery over the tiring-house.

The **players** could therefore create an interesting variety of exits and entrances, surprise their audience by disappearing below stage, reveal characters unexpectedly or fly in some special effect, or even an actor, from the Heavens. They could climb up to a balcony or appear on battlements by using the upper gallery. Musicians could also be placed there for a performance. And if members of the audience weren't enjoying themselves they could make their opinions clear very easily because no-one was far away from the stage.

The First Globe from the Hondius view of London, 1611.

THE SECOND GLOBE

After the fire which destroyed the **first Globe** the partnership of shareholders immediately set to and organized its rebuilding. These men had worked together since the formation of the **Lord Chamberlain's Men** in 1594: the **Burbage** brothers, Cuthbert and Richard; Shakespeare and four actors, Heminges, Condell, Ostler and Underwood. They had steered their company to considerable fame and fortune and their confidence is shown by the fact that they raised more money between them to rebuild the Globe than had been spent on any other **playhouse** – £1400. It was money well spent. The new theatre which opened in 1614 was described by an early visitor as 'the fayrest that ever was in England'.

Richard Burbage's father, James, had begun life as a carpenter before becoming a travelling **player** with the **Earl of Leicester's Men**. He would have performed throughout England on a simple, portable booth stage. James had gone on to run the first permanent playhouse and his sons carried on the family tradition in the two Globe theatres, acknowledged as the most splendid and practical in London. The **second Globe** continued in operation long after the death of Shakespeare in 1616 and of Richard Burbage in 1619. It was demolished in 1644, after an Act of Parliament of 1642 had closed the playhouses.

Visscher's engraving of London published in 1616, showing the Bear Garden and the Globe.

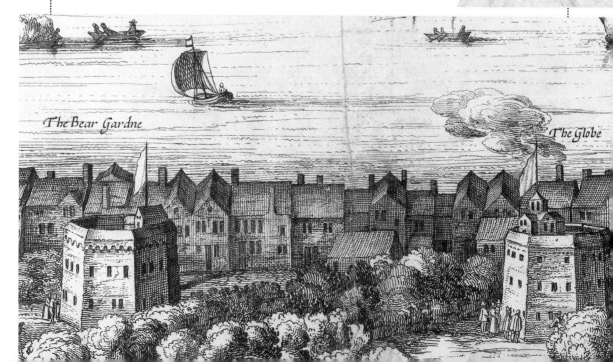

The Bear Gardne

The Globe

This engraving of the Second Globe was made in 1647. By mistake it was labelled *Beere Bayting*.

THE PURITAN OPPOSITION: THE END OF THE GLOBE

'... popular stage plays ... are sinful, ungodly spectacles.'

So wrote William Prynne in his book *Histrio Mastix*, published in 1632. Prynne was a **Puritan**, a member of a strict religious group which regarded pleasure of any kind as sinful. The Council of the City of London was dominated by Puritans throughout Shakespeare's career and they frequently made angry complaints about the corrupting effects of performances. If people saw murders on stage, wouldn't it make them violent? If servants were seen tricking their masters, wouldn't the audience turn criminal too? So ran the Puritan argument. They were also anxious about the opportunities playgoing might give for pickpockets and prostitutes to follow their trades, and for infectious diseases to spread. They were afraid that the large crowds at playhouses might become an unruly mob and threaten law and order.

Shakespeare pokes fun at the Puritans in the character of Malvolio in *Twelfth Night*. He is a kill-joy who is ridiculed and tricked unmercifully by the other characters.

By 1642, England was on the brink of civil war, with the Puritans led by Oliver Cromwell opposing King Charles I. Parliament then had its chance to close down the theatres completely and order the playhouses to be demolished. The Globe, where ambassadors and apprentices alike had seen the first performances of Shakespeare's plays, was forced out of action.

Theatre was not part of English life again until after the restoration of King Charles II in 1660.

INDOOR THEATRES

Since the thirteenth century boys at the cathedral schools, the royal chapels and the public schools had been performing plays, often translations of Latin comedies. What started as an educational exercise became a popular and commercially successful venture. The boy **players** were the first to perform in indoor **playhouses** and they attracted an enthusiastic audience.

JAMES BURBAGE'S BLACKFRIARS THEATRE

James Burbage, the impresario who had built the **Theatre**, was not a man to miss a trick. He had seen the success of the boys at their playhouse in Blackfriars, a fashionable residential part of London. In 1596 he bought a large hall in Blackfriars and converted it into a theatre for the **Chamberlain's Men**. This gave them a suitable place for winter performances. But local residents were not happy about having adult players on their doorstep and tried to ban them.

There were six main indoor playhouses in London but there is little detailed evidence about their size. The plays written for them, however, do provide some insight into how they were used and there are also some contemporary illustrations.

Several points of difference from performances in the public playhouses stand out.

• The use of lighting by candles and torches.

Middle Temple Hall where *Twelfth Night* was performed in 1602.

- More ghostly and other special visual effects.
- More music, sometimes played for up to an hour before the play started, and during the performance.
- More subtle forms of comedy, such as satire, which depended on a knowledgeable and sophisticated audience.
- Higher seat prices which in effect meant only the well-off could attend. Few tradesmen, and certainly none of their apprentices, would have been seen there.

Burbage's new playhouse was rectangular, with the stage at one end of a hall on the ground floor of the building. Most seats were in front of the stage but there were boxes at each side and on the stage balcony. The upper galleries curved round, so there was audience on four sides. It is probable that the **Blackfriars** held 600–700 people (the **Globe** held about 3000), plus fifteen gallants on stools on the stage itself.

The increased admission charges went with the reorganization of the audience. Those who had paid most sat nearest the stage: at the front, or in boxes at the side – little cubicles separating the lord and his guests from the mass of the audience. Most fashionable of all was a seat actually on the side of the stage, very popular with young noblemen who wanted to be seen. The glamour of the players rubbed off on them since they had to

An indoor performance with lavish scene decoration given by the Ballet Comique de la Royne, 1581.

collect their stools from the **tiring-house** at the back of the stage. Playgoers paying least sat at the back. This is still the arrangement in most theatres today.

The indoor playhouses catered for a more prosperous and fashionable audience than the outdoor theatres. From 1609 the **King's Men** played at the Blackfriars and the Globe, and so continued to entertain the whole range of Elizabethan society, but the idea of playing to a selected audience had taken root once and for all.

The Theatre and the Court

Private Performances

The companies enjoyed a third type of performance when they were invited to play at Court or in another great house to provide entertainment for the family's guests. Conditions here must have been similar to those in the indoor theatres but these special occasions gave the opportunity for even more spectacular effects.

The Revels Office

Entertainment was an important part of life at Court, and in the reign of Elizabeth's father, Henry VIII, a **Revels Office** was set up to organize shows and maintain a wardrobe of costumes. As the public theatre flourished during Elizabeth's reign the Revels Office began to control all theatre matters. Parliament was still in the early stages of its development and the Queen's small, hand-picked group of advisers – the Privy Council – was still the most powerful body. The chief officer was the **Lord Chamberlain**, and the **Master of the Revels** and his Revels Office was directly responsible to him.

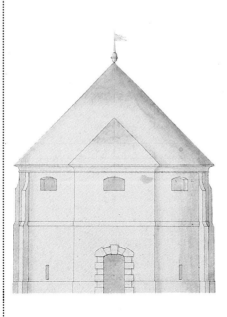

Plans for an indoor playhouse by Inigo Jones, possibly for the Cockpit, 1617.

The Master of the Revels licensed companies and had the pick of performances for Court entertainment. He also censored plays. This meant he checked them and could order sections to be cut out or performances banned if they offended against religious belief, or seemed not to give unquestioning obedience to the rule of law, the Government and the Queen. Censorship by the Lord Chamberlain's Office only came to an end in 1968!

PLAYING AT COURT

During Elizabeth's reign performances might be given in existing halls in the royal palaces – such as Hampton Court, Greenwich, Richmond or Windsor – or a purpose-built hall might be constructed for a special occasion.

The Great Hall at Hampton Court has a solid wooden screen standing 11 feet 6 inches (3.5 metres) in front of one of the end walls. Behind is a passageway leading to the kitchens. The screen has two doorways. A stage would have been built in front of the screen, and the doors covered with curtains to make a playing space similar to the stage in the public theatres. The Queen sat on a platform at the opposite end with guests seated along the length of the hall, leaving a further playing space in the middle. The Queen got the best view!

No expense or effort was spared in building a hall to honour and

An illustration to a play, *Roxana*, published in 1632, showing a performance taking place. The spectators seem to be sitting and this suggests an indoor playhouse, probably the Cockpit.

impress important foreign visitors. In 1581 the Duke of Alençon merited a specially designed banqueting hall at Whitehall where several plays were performed. It was highly decorated and included a canvas in the ceiling painted with clouds, stars and sunbeams. Three hundred and seventy-five men worked on the hall which was completed in three weeks and cost £1744.

COSTUME

The Elizabethans loved clothes. The Queen set the trend for all those with the money to follow, using rich fabrics decorated with lace, cloth of gold and even jewels, especially pearls. Fashions in style and colour changed as rapidly as they do today and the Elizabethans invented names for the latest shades: pepper, tobacco, sea-water and puke (a dark brown) were some of them.

The **players** had to match the leaders of fashion in the lavishness and variety of their costume for aristocratic characters. **Thomas Platter**, a Swiss visitor to the London theatres, noted in his diary in 1599 that noblemen often left their best clothes to their servants after their death. The servants benefited, not by wearing anything so grand but by selling them to the players. **Henslowe's** and **Alleyn's** papers show that they spent much more on costume than on stage properties. The amounts are amazingly high. For instance, Henslowe bought a 'black velvet cloak with sleeves embroidered all with silver and gold' for just over £20.

Henslowe's list of costume includes
- cloaks in scarlet with gold lace and buttons
- cloaks in purple satin decorated with silver
- a costume in copper lace, 'carnation' velvet, flame, ginger, red and green
- women's gowns of white satin and cloth of gold.

Richard Tarleton was a very popular comic actor. He is dressed ready for a performance here, very simply and with his pipe and drum.

It is as well that some players of poorer characters or servants could be simply and inexpensively dressed. They wore everyday clothes which they provided themselves.

HISTORICAL COSTUME

Some people attending performances of Shakespeare's plays today say that they want to see them in 'the proper dress'. They dislike productions which use modern twentieth-century costume or a mixture of styles. Yet the evidence suggests that Elizabethan players used basically 'modern dress': clothes of their own time with additions to indicate special characteristics or a particular historical period. There is no evidence of much attempt at historical accuracy.

The Peacham drawing of a performance of *Titus Andronicus* shows the leading character dressed in a drape rather like a Roman toga over a bodice and hose (leggings). The soldiers with him, however, are in Elizabethan dress. Henslowe's costume list is largely of contemporary Elizabethan dress although of a very rich, colourful and decorated kind. He includes a small number of specials:

- two Danish suits
- one coat for a Moor
- four Turks' heads
- 'the suit of motley for the Scotchman'

Players evidently enjoyed dressing up and Robert Greene, a poet, ridiculed them in *A Quip For An Upstart Courtier* (1592): the player wore a fur-trimmed gown 'laid thick on the sleeves with lace', and showed 'his white taffeta hose and black silk stockings'; the huge ruff around his neck made it look as if his head was in a 'wicker cage' topped by a 'little hat with brims'. A dedicated follower of fashion!

The first illustration of a Shakespeare play: a production of *Titus Andronicus*, c.1594.

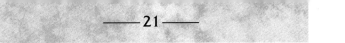

THE SYMBOLISM OF COSTUME AND COLOUR

The Elizabethan interest in design of all kinds was not just about decoration. They had a detailed sense of the connections between shape and colour and human experience. They also loved puzzles, clever jokes and wit of all kinds, including choice of clothes. For an Elizabethan audience the colour and style of costume worn on stage would have quite specific associations.

Hamlet wearing black – the colour of melancholy (sadness) – because he is mourning for his dead father is an obvious example. We would need help, though, to know that yellow was the colour worn by a lover, so when Malvolio is tricked into appearing in yellow stockings in *Twelfth Night* he is being cruelly led to believe that he is loved by Olivia. Doctors wore gowns of scarlet, lawyers' gowns were black, serving men wore blue coats, a cardinal (a senior Roman Catholic priest) wore rich scarlet but a humble monk or friar wore a rough habit of grey or brown. Women who had gone mad wore long-haired wigs.

Robert Armin, another popular clown (comic actor), dressed here in a long coat which suggested to an Elizabethan audience that he was playing a Fool.

Robert Armin, a popular actor in Shakespeare's company, is pictured here in a costume which had clear meaning for his audience. Instead of the fashionable short doublet and hose of a dashing young man he is wearing the long coat of a 'natural' fool, in other words of a simple, naive person. Shakespeare's plays contain references to clothes which emphasize their importance at the time. Polonius in *Hamlet* advises his son to make a good impression by dressing as well as he can, for 'the apparel oft proclaims the man'. Dogberry in *Much Ado About Nothing* boasts that he is a respectable, well-off man and gives his evidence: 'and one, moreover, that hath two coats'.

COSTUME IN THE HENSLOWE PAPERS

This illustration is of **Edward Alleyn** in one of his most admired roles, Tamburlaine, in Marlowe's play of the same name. Tamburlaine was a ruthless conqueror who had actually lived in the fourteenth century, rampaging around the eastern Mediterranean lands. He died 183 years before Alleyn first portrayed him on the stage of the **Rose**. Far from being dressed as a Scythian shepherd, which he was at first, or the ruthless medieval warlord, which he later became, this Tamburlaine is elegantly dressed like an Elizabethan gentleman. The one piece of special costume is the decorated sleeveless cloak over his jerkin. **Henslowe's** list of costumes included a coat with copper lace, for Tamburlaine.

HENSLOWE'S INVENTORY

The list includes some other exotic costumes: a 'fairy's gown of buckram' (a kind of coarse cloth), 'a pair of giant's hose' (leggings), and a ghost's suit. He also had in his wardrobe a bear's skin and head, a bull's head, a lion's skin and two lion's heads. Shakespeare introduces a bear in *The Winter's Tale* so presumably his company owned a bear skin too.

Here are some of the costumes described in Henslowe's own words, only the spelling has been modernized. A gown was a long loose costume.

Edward Alleyn dressed for the part of Tamburlaine in Christopher Marlowe's play of that name. He wore rich Elizabethan dress with a decorated sleeveless cloak on top.

GOWNS

1 Harry [Henry] VIII gown
2 the black velvet gown with white fur
3 a crimson robe striped with gold and faced with ermine [white fur]
4 one of wrought [decorated] cloth of gold
5 one of red silk with gold buttons
6 a cardinal's gown
7 women's gowns
and
16 angel's silk

PROPERTIES AND STAGE SETTING

Stage properties, known simply as **props**, are all the things which are used on stage, such as tables and benches with bottles and tankards in a tavern scene, or books and papers in a scene about business. **Players** also had personal props, things particularly used by their characters. Many of Shakespeare's characters need swords, daggers or sticks. Prospero in *The Tempest* has his magic staff. The witches in *Macbeth* need a cauldron. Malvolio in *Twelfth Night* has to have a ring to give to Cesario. Players might have chosen other bits and pieces which are not demanded by the text but which helped to show the personality of the character they played.

Shakespeare gives us a good idea of how props were used in the play-within-a-play in *A Midsummer Night's Dream*. Some workmen perform the tragic love story of *Pyramus and Thisbe*. The lovers are separated by a wall and a player comes on suitably kitted out to play the part:

'this loam and roughcast doth show That I am that same wall, the ... truth is so.'

Someone in the company must have enjoyed himself mixing mud and plaster to make himself look like a piece of wall. In the same play the Man-in-the-Moon has a dog, a lantern and a thorn bush – traditional belongings of this character.

STAGE PROPS AND PLAYERS' PROPS IN HENSLOWE'S INVENTORY

Thanks to **Henslowe's** methodical list-making we can see the resources of his theatre company. Many of the things he itemizes must have been associated with particular plays and sometimes we can have a good guess as to which one. Henslowe lists 'one Hell's mouth' which was probably used for performances of Marlowe's *Dr Faustus*. His company continued to perform this at the **Fortune** after they'd moved from the **Rose**, so it must have been a favourite with their audiences. An eye-witness account of a performance in 1620 sounds spectacular:

'a many may behold shagg-hayrd devils running roaring over the stage with squibs in their mouths, while drummers make thunder in the tiring-house ...'

Henslowe's list includes small things like,

'1 globe ... 1 pope's mitre ... 1 black dog ... 2 fans of feathers ...'

There are also much larger pieces of scenery or constructions such as

'the city of Rome ... 1 chain of dragons ... great horse ... wheel and frame in the Siege of London ...'

These things would have to be moved on and off, as would the hanging man in the illustration below of *The Spanish Tragedy*. Sometimes things could be 'discovered' behind the curtain of the alcove of the **tiring-house**. A trapdoor was obviously used: Shakespeare's company performed *A Warning for Fair Women* in which the trap was used to great effect – 'suddenly riseth up a great tree'.

The list of properties owned by the **Revels Office** is broadly similar to Henslowe's. The players must have enjoyed realistic detail and spectacular effects as part of their performances.

An illustration to the play *The Spanish Tragedy* by Thomas Kyd which shows a performance in which a flaming torch is used and a piece of scenery, an arch from which a character has been hung.

STYLE OF ACTING

Our evidence for understanding how the players performed is found mainly in **Henslowe's** papers, in the plays themselves, and in various accounts by members of the audience. We have quite a lot of information, which is summarized here.

- **Players** were expected to attend a brief rehearsal period for a new play and might be fined if they didn't turn up.
- Parts were written out with the cues (the lines spoken immediately before a particular character's speech), but no player would have had his own copy of the full play.
- There were no women on the Elizabethan stage. Women's parts were taken by boys or young men.
- Those playing the comic parts were notorious for improvising their own lines and jokes.

- There are many songs, dances and fights in the plays, so players must have had these skills.
- Many performances ended with a lively dance, a jig. A Swiss traveller reports that even the 'tragedy of the first emperor, Julius Caesar' ended in a dance: 'they danced as was their custom, very elegantly; two people in men's clothes and two in women's combining wonderfully with each other, gave this performance.'
- During performances the players were helped by a book-keeper, or prompter, probably sitting in the tiring-house following the text in his copy. He also put up a scheme of the action of the play so that as players came off stage into the **tiring-house** they could check what happened next.

Will Kempe dancing a jig. An illustration from an account of his famous 9 day dance from London to Norwich. Jigs were a popular part of stage performances particularly at the end of a play.

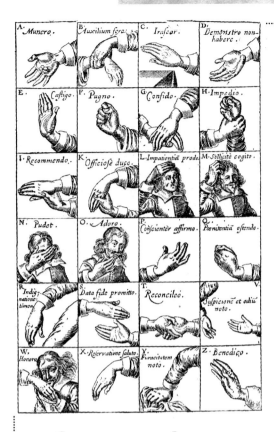

Illustrations of gestures. Sir Richard Baker, an Elizabethan play goer who saw Shakespeare's leading actor, Burbage, perform, said 'gracefulness of action is the greatest pleasure of a play'.

CONTEMPORARY ACCOUNTS

In Shakespeare's play, Prince Hamlet gives instructions to a group of players on how they should perform. His warning about the danger of overacting probably reflects Shakespeare's own views. Hamlet wanted a fluent way of speaking and a moderate use of gesture with no shouting or overdone vocal effects:

'Speak the speech, I pray you, as I pronounced it to you – trippingly on the tongue . . . Nor do not saw the air too much with your hand, thus, but use all gently . . . O, it offends me to the soul to hear a robustious fellow tear a passion to tatters ... to split the ears of the groundlings ....'

He also explains that the aim of acting is to show the audience what life and human emotion is actually like:

'Suit the action to the word, the word to the action . . . For anything so overdone is from the purpose of playing, whose end was and is to hold as 'twere the mirror up to nature, to show virtue her own feature, scorn her own image . . .'

A letter praising a performance of Shakespeare's *Othello,* at Oxford by the **King's Men** in September 1610, particularly admires the skill of the boy playing Desdemona, Othello's wife:

'They have acted with enormous applause to full houses ... They had tragedies . . . in which some things ... brought forth tears ... Moreover that famous Desdemona killed before us by her husband, although she always acted her whole part supremely well, yet when she was killed she was even more moving, for when she fell back upon the bed she implored the pity of the spectators by her very face.'

It seems that on this occasion the players of Shakespeare's company had achieved what Hamlet talked of.

REBUILDING SHAKESPEARE'S GLOBE

On 23 April 1988, a fascinating and ambitious project began to take shape: nothing less than the building of a copy of the **Globe** Theatre where Shakespeare worked for much of his career. Sam Wanamaker, a famous American film and stage actor with a passion for Shakespeare, was the man with the vision and energy behind the project. I was once told of a man who years earlier found himself in a pub in the centre of London being shown sketches and listening to an enthusiastic American, a complete stranger, talking about his dream of rebuilding the Globe; Wanamaker's plans had been brewing for a long time.

He had been raising support and money for several years before that day in April 1988 when the building began. Sadly Sam Wanamaker died in 1993 before it was complete but he left a dedicated group of architects, theatre historians, musicians and many well-known actors including his daughter, Zoe Wanemaker, who are continuing the project.

Sam Wanamaker's enthusiasm inspired support around the world and the organization he set up is called the International Shakespeare Globe Centre. The reconstructed theatre is not meant to be just a museum or an elaborate monument to a dead poet: when it is finished and stands on the South Bank in London, near its original site, it will be a place for practical research.

Building the new Globe, which forms part of the International Shakespeare Globe Centre due to be complete in 1999.

The Royal Shakespeare Company's Swan theatre in Stratford upon Avon.

stage in sunlight or shadow? Did some of the audience sit on the stage itself as they did in the indoor theatres? Key questions like this are being explored.

"The Globe project has no skeletons. (Its life) will not be a matter of resurrecting old bones but of the excitement of modern discovery, a new life for old plays."

Performances of Shakespeare's plays will be given in conditions which mirror the Elizabethan theatre: natural light, live sound and music, an open roof, audience packed close to the stage.

Extensive research and historical detective work was needed before the new Globe's architect, Theo Crosby, could finalize his design. Sam Wanamaker praised the architect's skill as "chief negotiator between the demands of the scholars and the demands of practicality". There are few surviving records or references to the Globe and they are often contradictory. Was the theatre round, hexagonal (six-sided) or polygonal (many-sided)? Was the

A few other theatres designed this century have tried to find the intimacy of the first **playhouses**, notably the Royal Shakespeare Company's **Swan** theatre in Stratford upon Avon. Actors, directors and designers working there have discovered the challenges and opportunities of close links between stage and audience; on three sides at stage level and in galleries above the actors' heads. Elizabethan theatre gave and demanded an intense, energetic and often highly-charged relationship between performer and audience. Elizabethan and Jacobean plays come alive in this act of sharing.

GLOSSARY

Groundling A spectator who paid one (old) penny and stood in the yard, the area nearest the stage.

Heavens A ceiling above the acting area of an outdoor playhouse to protect the actors from bad weather, often painted blue with silver stars.

Master of the Revels An official who ran the **Revels Office** and prevented plays from being performed which might, in his view, cause riots or offend the monarch or other important people.

Player An actor

Playhouse A theatre

Poet A writer of plays

Props Stage properties: all things used on stage by players, such as books, purses, letters, swords.

Puritan A person whose religious beliefs led to a strict view of what was right and wrong, and who opposed the theatre and other public entertainments because they might encourage wrong doing. Puritans become powerful in London and in Parliament. Their influence directly led to the closing of the theatres in 1642.

Revels Office A government office responsible for court entertainments. Among other things it had a wardrobe of clothes available for plays.

Tiring-house A theatre dressing-room behind the stage.

Other **bold** words in the text are theatres, theatre companies and key people.

REFERENCE

Further reading

Heinemann Our World series: *Shakespeare and Theatre*
The Heinemann Shakespeare series
The Heinemann Advanced Shakespeare series
Court, Crowd and Playhouse by Francois Laroque (Thames and Hudson)
Playgoing in Shakespeare's London by Andrew Gurr
(Cambridge University Press)
Rebuilding Shakespeare's Globe (Wiedenweld and Nicholson)

Models

The Globe Theatre – A card model kit of the reconstructed
Globe theatre at Bankside, London

Places to visit

Shakespeare's Globe Exhibition
New Globe Walk
Bankside
Southwark
London SE1 9EB

Telephone: London – 928 6406

Anne Hathaway's Cottage
Shottery
Stratford upon Avon

Mary Arden's House and The Shakespeare Countryside Museum
Wilmcote
Stratford upon Avon

The Shakespeare Centre
39 Henley Street
Stratford upon Avon

INDEX